Dear Parent:
Your child's love of reading starts here!

Every child learns to read in a different way and at his or her own speed. You can help your young reader improve and become more confident by encouraging his or her own interests and abilities. You can also guide your child's spiritual development by reading stories with biblical values and Bible stories, like I Can Read! books published by Zonderkidz. From books your child reads with you to the first books he or she reads alone, there are I Can Read! books for every stage of reading:

SHARED READING
Basic language, word repetition, and whimsical illustrations, ideal for sharing with your emergent reader.

BEGINNING READING
Short sentences, familiar words, and simple concepts for children eager to read on their own.

READING WITH HELP
Engaging stories, longer sentences, and language play for developing readers.

READING ALONE
Complex plots, challenging vocabulary, and high-interest topics for the independent reader.

ADVANCED READING
Short paragraphs, chapters, and exciting themes for the perfect bridge to chapter books.

I Can Read! books have introduced children to the joy of reading since 1957. Featuring award-winning authors and illustrators and a fabulous cast of beloved characters, I Can Read! books set the standard for beginning readers.

A lifetime of discovery begins with the magical words **"I Can Read!"**

Visit www.icanread.com for information on enriching your child's reading experience.
Visit www.zonderkidz.com for more Zonderkidz I Can Read! titles.

Lord, you have made so many things!
How wise you were when you made all of them!
The earth is full of your creatures.
—*Psalm 104:23–25*

ZONDERKIDZ

Cats, Dogs, Hamsters, and Horses
Copyright © 2010 by Zonderkidz

Requests for information should be addressed to:
Zonderkidz, *Grand Rapids, Michigan 49530*

Library of Congress Cataloging-in-Publication Data

Cats, dogs, hamsters, and horses.
    p. cm. — (I can read!)
        ISBN 978-0-310-72009-6 (softcover)
    1. Pets—Religious aspects—Christianity—Juvenile literature.
BT746.C38 2010
231.7'65—dc22   2009048440

Editor: Mary Hassinger
Art direction & design: Sarah Molegraaf

Printed in China

11 12 13 14 15 /SCC/ 10 9 8 7 6 5 4 3 2

ZONDER**kidz**

· · · MADE·BY·GOD · · ·

Cats, Dogs, Hamsters, and Horses

CONTENTS

God made all animals.

Some animals

have become friends for people.

One special animal pet is called a…

CAT!

God made about forty different
kinds of cats.

Some are called Persian and Siamese.

Cats have different characteristics.

Persians have long, flowing coats
and flat faces.

Siamese have creamy-colored short
coats with darker ears, paws, and tails.

All cats have strong teeth and jaws,
good hearing, and can see well
in the dark.

Most cats live ten to fifteen years.

To keep a cat happy and healthy

people feed them a good diet

with vitamins and minerals.

Cats like to drink water.

People think milk is a good drink

for cats. But be careful!

Many cats get sick

if they drink cow's milk.

Cats need doctor visits just like people.
But cats help take care of
themselves too. They clean
their fur by licking.
Cats use their tongues, which feel
like sandpaper, to do this job.

Cats let people know how they feel.

When cats are happy, they purr.

When cats are upset, they hiss
and can scratch.

If a cat gets nervous, you might
see its tail or ears twitch.

Cats love to play.

Cats like yarn, bells, and catnip.

They also like to just be petted.

God made all animals.

Some animals

have become friends for people.

One special animal pet is called a…

DOG!

Many people have dogs as pets.
God made many breeds of dogs—
so many that it is difficult to count.
Some kinds of dogs are Labradors
and Chihuahuas.

Some dogs make good friends
for families.
These dogs are taught to be gentle
and behave well.
They can be protective and love
to run and play.

Some dogs learn special skills.

They help people live safely

and do their jobs.

Some dogs help people who cannot

see or hear well.

Other dogs help police find

lost people or things.

People who have dogs feed them diets with vitamins and minerals. Some dogs love to share people food, but it is not always healthy!

People can train their dogs

to do tricks.

Some people take their dog to school.

But don't forget, dogs love to

play too!

God made all animals.

Some animals

have become friends for people.

One special animal pet is called a…

HAMSTER!

God made many kinds of hamsters.

Some hamsters that make

good pets are Dwarf, Teddy Bear,

and Panda hamsters.

These can all be found at pet shops

along with supplies they need

to stay healthy and safe.

Hamsters have poor eyesight.

Since many live in burrows,

it is fine for them.

Even if hamsters live in cages

they like to burrow under

torn-up paper and cardboard tubes.

Hamsters have good hearing, and

their noses work great too.

People keep their pet hamsters healthy
with good food and fresh water.
If they get sick, a veterinarian
can care for a hamster.

To help a hamster stay healthy, people make sure the hamster has a clean cage and an exercise wheel for running. People even get clear exercise balls for their hamster to roll and ride in.

Hamsters have large front teeth
that keep growing.
They must have things to
chew on, like hamster-safe sticks
and even dog biscuits.
These help their teeth stay short.

God made all animals.

Some animals

have become friends for people.

One special animal pet is called a…

HORSE!

There are more than 300 breeds
of horses in the world.
God made every one!
People had horses before Jesus was
born, more than 3,000 years before.
There are cave drawings and bones
in museums to show us.

People used horses for work
and transportation long ago.

Farmers used horses to plow or ride.

Others used horses to pull carriages.

Today, people have horses for work
and enjoyment.

People who have horses feed them
foods with vitamins and minerals,
like oats, hay, and special grains.
Some horses get treats
like sugar and apples.
Horses need lots of water every day.

Horses let their owners know
how they feel.

The way a horse moves its body
can show whether it is happy,
upset, or scared and startled.

A horse will be a happy pet as long as
its owner cares for and loves it,
grooms and feeds it, and makes sure
it has plenty of exercise and rest.